Rules For Judging And Suggestions To Schedule-makers, Judges, & Exhibitors

Royal Horticultural Society (Great Britain)

1899 CODE

RULES FOR JUDGING

AND

SUGGESTIONS

TO

SCHEDULE-MAKERS, JUDGES, & EXHIBITORS

DRAWN UP BY A COMMITTEE OF THE

Royal Horticultural Society

AND ISSUED BY ORDER OF THE COUNCIL

FOR USE AT

HORTICULTURAL EXHIBITIONS

SECOND EDITION, REVISED

COPYRIGHT

Printed for the Royal Horticultural Society

BY

SPOTTISWOODE & CO, NEW-STREET SQUARE, LONDON

1899

Q 135591

Judging Rules Committee.
'1896.

C. E. SHEA, Esq., *Chairman.*

Messrs. A. F. BARRON, V.M.H.	Messrs. J. McINDOE, V.M.H.
W. BENNETT	W. MARSHALL
P. BLAIR	F. W. MOORE
G. BUNYARD, V.M.H.	A. OUTRAM
A. DEAN	GEO. PAUL, V.M.H.
J. DOUGLAS	JAS. SMITH, V.M.H.
MALCOLM DUNN, V.M.H.	OWEN THOMAS, V.M.H.
BRUCE FINDLAY	D. THOMSON, V.M.H.
G. GORDON, V.M.H.	S. T. WRIGHT
J. LAING, V.M.H.	JOHN WRIGHT, V.M.H.

Rev. W. WILKS, M.A., *Secretary.*

NOTE.—The following gentlemen, though not actually on the Committee (owing chiefly to their distance from London), have been most kind in rendering valuable assistance in special departments :—

Rev. H. D'OMBRAIN	Messrs J. HARKNESS	Messrs. F. SANDER
Rev. H. FOSTER MELLIAR	H. J. JONES	A. W SUTTON
Messrs E BECKETT	E. MAWLEY	H. J. VEITCH
J. BURRELL	E. MOLYNEUX	C. J. WAITE
J. CYPHER	JAMES O'BRIEN	J. WARD
R DEAN	A H. PEARSON	W. WILLIAMSON
O. FIDLER	S. PERKINS	G. WOODWARD
JOHN FRASER	W. POPE	G. WYTHES

PREFACE
1896.

—•◆•—

In formulating the following Rules of Judging, the Royal Horticultural Society endeavours to meet a need, which has long been
felt, that the principles whereon the judging of Fruits, Vegetables, Plants, and Flowers proceeds, should be systematised;
and, as far as possible, embodied in a Code, which may find
acceptance at the hands of those who are called upon to act as
Judges.

It is not suggested that the Rules now proposed can be
regarded as final. Doubtless, experience will suggest, and the
inevitable modification of essential conditions will, from time to
time, compel, amendment of the Code. It is, however, hoped that
the following Rules and Suggestions may be in themselves of
some general use, and also form the beginning and basis of a
Code which may before long be arrived at, which will be regarded
as authoritative by reason of the universality of its adoption.
The Council of the Royal Horticultural Society will be glad to
receive suggestions of improvements and emendations, and a
note of any omissions, for the correction of future editions.

Very great difficulty has been experienced in arriving at any
distinct conclusion with regard to the words "kind" and
"variety"; the "Brassica Family"; "Hardy Plants"; and the
term "Amateur"; and it is not pretended that the results even
now are in all respects quite satisfactory.

As far as possible uniformity, or at least consistency, of
principle has been sought to be attained, so that the Rules may
be harmonious. The principle of Pointing adopted aims at
bringing the values of the several recognised attributes of
excellence into strict relation one to another; thereby presenting
a definite System of Judging, instead of one necessarily varying,

as at present, with the varying preferences of individual Judges. It is hoped that not only will the less experienced be guided, but that the creation of Standards of excellence will also materially assist the exhibitor in the cultivation and staging of his productions.

Too great stress cannot be laid upon the necessity which exists that Schedules should be framed with the utmost care and exactness. Too frequently indefiniteness, or looseness and ambiguity of expression in the Schedule, are to be held responsible for much of the dissatisfaction which so often attends competitive exhibitions. Schedule-makers are, therefore, strongly urged to consider carefully the suggestions and recommendations which accompany the Rules of Judging.

It will be noticed that in order to provide an elasticity of "pointing" commensurate with the several detailed aspects of excellence recognisable in the flower, plant, fruit, or vegetable, an extended number of "points" has been recommended. It is not, however, suggested that, in the practical work of judging, the experienced Judge will often find it necessary to go, in detail, through the form of estimating each separate item upon the basis given. But the system, and principle, laid down should, nevertheless, govern the general action of Judges, and will, in case of difference of opinion, furnish the basis whereon the ultimate decision must rest.

An endeavour was made to form an Index to the whole, but it was soon found that, to be of any real value, the Index would be almost as long as the Code; it was, therefore, for the present abandoned, a short Table of Contents being prefixed instead.

In order to simplify reference to this Code, the paragraphs are numbered seriatim throughout.

NOTE TO SECOND EDITION, 1899.

The only important alteration from the 1896 Code will be found embodied in paragraphs 7, 7A, 7B, 8, 46, and 50; an Appendix has been drawn up on Point-Judging and Point-Value; and the Society's list of Culinary and Dessert Fruits has also been added.

W. WILKS, Sec. R.H.S.

CONTENTS.

HORTICULTURAL EXHIBITIONS.

1899 CODE.

GENERAL RULES.

1. Any prize may, at the discretion of the Judges, be withheld or modified if the exhibit be considered undeserving the prize offered.

2. All exhibits should be correctly and distinctly named. Errors in naming do not actually disqualify, but Judges should recognise correctness and distinctness of naming as telling in favour of an exhibitor in a close competition.

3. The words kind and **variety** are used in the following sense, viz.: Peaches, Nectarines, Apples, Plums, are, for exhibition purposes, distinct **kinds** of Fruit; Peas, Cabbages, Kales, Savoys, Brussels Sprouts, Carrots, Broad Beans, and Kidney Beans, are distinct **kinds** of Vegetables; Roses, Chrysanthemums, Phloxes, are distinct **kinds** of Flowers. Royal George, Noblesse, Alexander, are distinct **varieties** of Peaches; Mrs. J. Laing, Marie Baumann, A. K. Williams, are distinct **varieties** of Roses; American Wonder, Duke of Albany, Ne Plus Ultra, are distinct **varieties** of Peas; and so on. §§ 50, 72, 73, 170–175.

As a general rule, for the purpose of exhibiting, all natural *genera* are **kinds**, and all variations within a genus are **varieties.** Peaches and Nectarines and the Cabbage tribe are notable exceptions to this; Black and White Grapes are also for exhibition allowed as distinct **kinds** of fruit. §§ 50, 72, 73.

In collections of vegetables of distinct kinds Schedule-makers are particularly warned that it will be necessary to word classes for collections somewhat thus: " Class ——. Collection of Vegetables, six distinct kinds (only one* of the Cabbage Tribe may be included) "—for if such a note be not added the exhibitor would be at liberty to show White Cabbage, Red Cabbage, Kale, Savoys, and Brussels Sprouts as five of the six kinds required. § 73.

4. All exhibits *for prizes* must have been grown by the exhibitor or his employer for at least *two months* before the date

* Or " two," if it is desired to permit two.

of the Exhibition, unless the Schedule make distinct exception. This does not necessarily apply to Flowers for bouquets and table decorations, which may be purchased for the purpose, unless the Schedule forbid ; but they must always be set up and arranged by the Exhibitor. The purchase of Flowers ready arranged disqualifies an Exhibitor.

5. *Two or more* persons may not exhibit for prizes separately from the *same* garden, nursery, or plant-house.

6. In the case of two exhibits being adjudged "Equal First," the 1st and 2nd prizes should be divided between the winners, the next in order of merit taking the 3rd prize. Precisely the same principle applies to an "Equal Second," in which case there will be no 3rd prize. If two competitors are "Equal Third," either a duplicate 3rd must be given or the 3rd prize may be divided between them.

7. If a particular number of plants, flowers, fruits, or vegetables is specified for a class, dish, or collection, any excess or deficiency in the number disqualifies an exhibitor. Judges have no power to correct the mistake of an exhibitor. Nevertheless,

7A. Judges, if unanimous, may point out to the Referee, Secretary, or Manager of a Show, any slight departures from the exact terms of the Schedule, which, in their opinion, are the result of accident (such as misplacement of fruits or foliage, error in number, &c.), and are merely technical, not substantially affecting the character or merit of the exhibit, and obviously not made with "intention to deceive." § 38.

7B. The Referee, Secretary, or Manager, having had his attention thus called by the Judges to any such slight incorrectness, has the power (with the sanction of the Judges, but not otherwise) either to give the exhibitor (if nigh at hand) opportunity to make the necessary correction or to correct it himself to the best of his ability.

8. Any exhibits contrary to the *wording* of the Schedule (unremedied under §§ 7, 7A, 7B,) are disqualified ; but, in the case of an exhibitor having made a disqualifying error, through misunderstanding the terms of the Schedule or such other innocent cause, the Judges, though forced to disqualify, may recommend the authorities to grant an extra prize if they consider the exhibit sufficiently meritorious.

9. As regards the relative merit of the exhibits the decision

of the Judges is final; but in case of any objection to the interpretation of the wording of the Schedule, no prize shall be paid until the matter under dispute has been referred to the Committee of the Show, or other authority.

10. Any protest or other objection must be made in writing, and be handed to the Secretary of the Show.

11. With the exception of an objection based upon alleged fraud, every protest must be lodged within two hours of the opening of the Show to the public.

12 The Council of the Royal Horticultural Society is willing to act as Referee in cases of dispute, if the parties concerned signify their consent to abide by the Council's decision, in which case a complete Schedule must be sent, with a statement from both sides, accompanied by a fee of 10s. 6d.

13. No person shall be allowed to compete as an *amateur* who sells *plants* (except when giving up possession of the place where they grow, or in the case of new seedlings or sports), *grafts, cuttings, or buds for budding*, nor any person in the employ of a nurseryman. Any objection raised as to the rightful qualification of an exhibitor shall be referred to the Committee or other authority for arbitration, and their decision shall be final and binding on both parties.

The term " Amateur " is here employed in its broadest sense, that is, in contradistinction to "nurseryman." In some Schedules the word is used more strictly, denoting an amateur *gardener, i.e.*, one who employs *no* professional help whatever in the cultivation of his garden, in contradistinction to an amateur *owner*, who cultivates by means of professional gardeners in his employment.

14. No exhibitor may take more than *one prize* in the same class, unless specially permitted by the Schedule.

15. The place of exhibition should be cleared of everyone, except duly authorised persons, previous to the Judges commencing their duties , and the Secretary, or the Stewards, or other duly appointed persons should see that each exhibit has its proper card duly affixed.

16. Judging should commence **punctually** at the time appointed, and the rule fixing the time for the conclusion of staging should be **strictly enforced.**

17. No Judge must have any interest whatever in the class or classes in which he is appointed to officiate.

SUGGESTIONS TO SCHEDULE-MAKERS.

See also §§ 3, 36, 42, 73, 91, 143, 159, 165–175.

18. State clearly at what hour exhibitors can begin and must finish staging, and at what hour they may remove their exhibits.

19. State clearly at what hour (*a*) subscribers, and (*b*) the public will be admitted, and at what hour the Show closes.

20. Adhere strictly and exactly to all hours stated and notices publicly given. § 16.

21. Alterations in the arrangements should be avoided, except in cases of actual necessity, and then every possible means of publicity should be resorted to for making them generally known.

22. The Rules and Regulations under which the Show is held cannot be too clearly and plainly stated. All should be printed together, and the exhibitor's attention prominently drawn to the page on which this is done. Where it is intended that this R.H.S. Code should apply, it should be distinctly so stated in the Schedule; *e.g., Judging will be conducted under the R.H.S. 1899 Code of Rules.*

23. Every Schedule should contain a paragraph similar to the following :—" All exhibitors for prizes must conform strictly to the ' Regulations ' on page —."

24. Except in cases where the Point-Value system is adopted (p. 44), it is advised that in the apportionment of the prize-money the system expressed by the figures 3, 2, 1 be used. In putting this system into effect, the easiest way is to fix first on the amount of the 3rd prize in any class, and then double that amount for the 2nd prize, and then add together the 2nd and 3rd for the 1st prize. Let the 3rd prize be always fixed at an even shilling or sixpence, and no difficulty can occur in carrying the 3, 2, 1 system into effect. For instance :

If the 3rd prize is fixed at 10*s.*, the 2nd will be £1, and the 1st £1. 10*s.* Total, £3.

If the 3rd prize is fixed at 3*s.* 6*d.*, the 2nd will be 7*s.*, and the 1st 10*s.* 6*d.* Total, £1. 1*s.*

If the 3rd prize is fixed at 2*s.*, the 2nd will be 4*s.*, and the 1st 6*s.* Total, 12*s.*

25. When there is a class in which several items of one kind are asked for, and another class in which a less number of items

of the same kind are asked for, then the total sum apportioned to each of these classes should be in proportion to the *number* of items in each class. For example, if £4. 10s. is apportioned to a class for 9 dishes of Pears, then £3 should be apportioned to a class for 6 dishes, £1. 10s. for 3 dishes, and 10s. for 1 dish ; and so in all similar cases.

26. Schedules should very carefully distinguish between dessert and culinary fruits (p. 47) when such distinction is intended to be observed, and in classes in which it is required that the fruit should be *ripe* it should be *expressly so stated* in the Schedule. § 55.

27. Exhibitors' cards should contain on the " face " side the number and description of the class, with the name and address of the owner of the produce, also the name of the gardener (if any). The " back " of the card should contain the class number and exhibitor's number, for the guidance of the Judges. It is convenient, and often saves the Judges much time, if the colour of the cards is different for different Divisions. (*See* p. 52.) Suitable cards should also be provided for the Judges. (*See* p. 54.)

28. *Examples of how Classes for Collections of Fruit and Vegetables should be stated in the Schedule.*

   i. Collection of twelve dishes of Ripe Fruit; not less than six kinds, nor more than two varieties of a kind.

   ii. Plums, four dishes of dessert, distinct.

   iii. Collection of six distinct kinds of Vegetables ; only one of the Cabbage tribe may be included.

   iv. Collection of twelve Vegetables, not less than eight distinct kinds ; two of the Cabbage tribe only allowed.

   v. Collection of Potatos, twelve distinct varieties, 6 Round and 6 Kidney.

   vi. Potatos, single dish, one variety.

   vii. Peas, single dish, one variety.

N.B.—The number forming a dish should always be stated.

Examples to **avoid.**

  viii. Collection of Fruit, twelve sorts.

   ix. Four dishes of Plums.

    x. Collection of Vegetables.

   xi. Collection of Vegetables, distinct varieties.

  xii. Potatos, single dish.

SUGGESTIONS TO JUDGES.

29. Read carefully the Regulations and Conditions printed in the Schedule, and note any peculiar or unusual stipulations.

30. Note the number of competitors in each class, and take a general survey of the exhibits.

31. First dismiss from consideration all exhibits which are *manifestly inferior*. Then compare those which remain. Where the exhibits show unmistakable difference it is not necessary to judge by points. See Appendix, p. 43.

32. If there be any doubt as to the order of merit the Judges should critically examine each item of the exhibit, one of them calling out the number of points he suggests, and any Judge disagreeing should at once urge his own view of the case. Agreement having thus been arrived at, the total number of points will determine the order of merit.

33. Should the total number of points in any case be equal, and it be impossible (as, *e.g.*, in the case of a cup) to return an award of equality, effective arrangement and correct naming must determine the issue. § 2.

34. If a recount is necessary, special regard should be had to the relative value or difficulty of cultivation of the different kinds or varieties exhibited. Points may be given for evenness of size or beauty of arrangement.

35. If the Judges, being even in number, are unable to agree, they should call in some properly qualified person to decide between them, and at once abide by his casting-vote.

36. When the relative merits of the exhibits in any class have been determined, the words " First," " Second," " Third " should be plainly marked by one of the Judges on the back of the winning exhibitor's card (p. 53), and an official record kept, to be handed in to the Secretary of the Show. It is recommended that gummed prize-labels should be used and affixed to the cards (or the words stamped thereon) as the judging proceeds.

37. Judges should encourage good exhibits below the prize-winners by awarding a " Highly Commended " card in such cases.

38. Judges should not disqualify exhibits without a substantial reason, but when they are satisfied that there has been an intention to deceive, or that the conditions of the Schedule have been purposely violated, they should not hesitate for a moment; but see § 7A.

JUDGING FRUIT

39. By the word **dish** is understood any stand or receptacle, of any material, and of any shape. The word is used only to indicate the aggregation of a certain definite number or quantity of fruits, constituting together one individual item.

40. Every dish must consist of one variety only, unless the wording of the Schedule permit mixed dishes.

41. Unless otherwise specified, *a dish* is held to consist of—

1 Pineapple.

1 Melon.

2 or 3 Bunches of Grapes, as specified in the Schedule.

6 Peaches.

6 Nectarines.

9 Figs.

9 Apricots.

9 Plums.

6 Pears.

6 Apples.

6 Quinces.

12 Bananas.

6 Oranges.

*9 Dessert Tomatos, or 6 Bunches of the smaller varieties.

20 Strawberries.

50 Cherries.

50 Raspberries.

30 Gooseberries.

30 Bunches of Red, White, or Black Currants ; or

1 Pint of Black Currants (single berries).

30 Damsons, Prunes, or Bullaces.

1 Pound of Nuts.

* Tomatos are only recognised as Dessert Fruits where specifically admitted by the particular Schedule, thus : " *Tomatos admissible.*"

42. If it is wished to have a larger number of fruits to a dish than above mentioned, the Schedule should either (*a*) state the exact number required, or (*b*) say " Not more than —— fruits to a dish," or (*c*) give the size of basket or dish which may be used—*e.g.* : " Collection of Apples, distinct varieties, in dishes or baskets, not exceeding 15 inches in diameter if circular, or 19 by 15 inches if rectangular."

43. By " grown in the open air " it must be understood that

the plants or trees have flowered, and also set their fruit, as well as ripened it, without any other protection beyond netting or a coped wall.

Standards of Quality.

44. All fruits should be somewhat above the average size of the particular variety, and perfect in colour, form, and condition. Enormous specimens should not be preferred, as beyond a certain point, size may become a defect, especially in dessert fruits.

45. Varieties naturally large, but usually somewhat lacking in quality, should not be preferred to varieties naturally smaller but of greater recognised excellence.

46. Colour is often a decided addition to Apples, Pears, and Peaches ; but colour produced by rubbing off the natural bloom of the fruit, or by polishing it with milk or oil, or in any other way, should count against rather than in favour of an exhibit. In all cases—with Apples and Pears no less than with Grapes and Plums and Figs—the preservation of the natural bloom upon the surface of the fruit is greatly to be desired. Varieties naturally high coloured but lacking in flavour should, however, not be preferred to those naturally less coloured but of excellent flavour, *e.g.*, Alexandra Noblesse peach. Judges should bear in mind that size, colour, and shape are all comparative, whilst flavour and quality are absolute merits.

47. Where prizes are given " for flavour," the fruit *must* be tasted, but Judges should decline to taste specimens that are not of at least fair size and appearance.

48 Malformed fruit, spots, insect marks, bruises, decay, and want of stalks or eyes are defects.

49. In judging "Collections," regard must be paid to the relative importance of the different kinds, as well as to high cultivation, superior finish, and tasteful arrangement. Fruit should always be named. § 2.

50. It should be the rule in judging collections of miscellaneous fruits that where more than one dish of any one kind is present, each such dish should be appraised at its point-value separately. The lumping of dishes of the same kind in pointing is quite inadequate.

The relative importance of various kinds is indicated by

the number of points to be allotted to a perfect dish of each :—

	Points		Points
Pineapples . . .	10	Oranges . . .	6
*Muscat of Alexandria		Strawberries	6
Grapes . . .	10	Cherries . . .	5
Other White Grapes .	9	Gooseberries . .	5
†Black Grapes . .	9	Raspberries . .	5
Melons . . .	8	Currants . . .	4
Peaches . . .	8	Damsons . . .	4
Nectarines . . .	8	Cob Nuts and Filberts	4
Pears	8	Tomatos (if admitted)	4
Bananas . . .	8	Walnuts . . .	3
Apples . . .	7	Mulberries . . .	3
Figs	7	Medlars . . .	3
Plums . .	6	Blackberries (Brambles)	3
Apricots . . .	6		

* In judging Grapes, other things being equal, Muscat of Alexandria should receive, as above, one point more than other White Grapes.

† For the purposes of exhibiting, Black and White Grapes are considered distinct " kinds " of fruit (§ 3).

51. In case of equality extra points may, if necessary, be given for tasteful arrangement.

KINDS OF FRUIT.

52. *Grapes.*—The bunches should be of uniform size, of perfect shape, properly thinned so that every berry has had room to develop ; the bunch when cut remaining firm and compact. Large bunches with berries of varying size are less meritorious than smaller bunches with berries of a uniform size. The berries should be large *for the variety*, and carry a dense bloom. Loose bunches, ill-coloured berries, rubbing, shanking, spot, insect marks, and mildew are all grave defects.

For exhibition purposes Bowood Muscat, Charlesworth To-quay, and Tyninghame Muscat are to be regarded as synonymous with Muscat of Alexandria, and cannot be shown as distinct varieties. In the same way Gros Maroc and Cooper's Black are considered synonymous.

53. *Peaches and Nectarines.*—Large specimens of any variety

are generally of better flavour than small fruits of the same. They should display the colour natural to the variety, and be free from blemish of every kind. Split stones are a great defect.

54. *Apricots.*—High colour indicates high quality, the fruits should be evenly ripened on both sides.

55. *Apples and Pears for Dessert.*—These must be judged from the known flavour of the variety. They must be of good colour and appearance, but mere size should not outweigh quality. Unless the word "Ripe" occur in the Schedule in connection with Apples and Pears, the fruit may be shown ripe or unripe.

Apples and Pears for Cooking.—Size is a merit, if it be added to good quality. The fruit should have a clear skin and even outline. Deeply set stalks and eyes, and other irregularities of surface, which cause loss of time and waste in paring, are defects.

Although any Pear may be stewed, the term "Cooking" or "Stewing" Pears refers to recognised varieties which, as a rule, do not become melting until cooked, as, *e.g.*, Catillac, Uvedale's St. Germain, and others of the same nature.

56. *Bananas.*—The individual fruits must be large, clear and clean in the skin, thoroughly ripe, and of high flavour.

57. *Oranges.*—These must be well grown, even in size, clear in the skin, juicy, ripe, and of good flavour. They should always be shown with foliage attached.

58. *Melons.*—The fruits, which should be about 18 (and not less than 15) inches in circumference, must be cut and tasted. The flesh must be rich in flavour, melting and juicy; the fruit thick in the edible part, and thin in the rind. Scent is not a sufficient guide for determining condition and quality.

59. *Plums.*—Size, considering the variety and its flavour, is a merit—not mere size regardless of variety. The fruits should carry a good bloom.

60. *Figs.*—Size, considering the variety and its flavour, is a merit—not mere size. A slightly cracked skin, a juicy eye, and a fine bloom generally indicate good flavour.

61. *Cherries.*—Flavour, size, and brilliancy are the chief points. Shrivelled stalks are a blemish.

62. *Pineapples.*—These should be ripe throughout; even in size of pip, and regular in shape; the crown fresh, and in size

duly proportioned to the fruit, neither dwarfing it nor appearing insignificant.

63. *Currants.*—It is essential that Red and White Currants be shown in bunches as grown. The berries should be large, clean, brilliant and clear; the bunches well filled.

Black Currants may be shown in bunches or as single picked berries, which should be large and jet black.

64. *Gooseberries.*—Ripe fruit should be judged by flavour, in conjunction with freshness, size, and cleanliness; unripe Gooseberries for uniformity of size, and freshness.

65. *Strawberries and Raspberries.*—Ripeness and freshness should always accompany rich flavour, bright colour, and handsome shape and size. The fruits must be shown on the stalk.

66. *Tomatos* are sometimes allowed to be shown as dessert fruit, in which case they should be shown as small single fruits, or in bunches, and be judged by flavour. They should be thoroughly ripe, and bright red or yellow, without spot or blemish

JUDGING VEGETABLES.

67. All vegetables should be perfectly clean and fresh; free from blemish of any kind, and correctly named.   § 2.

68. Quality, coupled with a *size suitable for table use*, are the points of paramount importance in vegetables. Size, beyond that which invests the produce with the greatest value for table, cannot be regarded as meritorious, as it indicates coarseness, and must, therefore, be reckoned as a defect.

69. In cases of doubt as to whether (other things being equal) size or quality should be preferred, it is suggested that with cottagers' produce size may not inappropriately take the precedence, but in all gardeners' classes, where the most finished examples of culture for table use are expected, quality should be the leading feature in determining the award.

70. The samples composing "a dish" should be all of one size; and of one variety only.

71. In judging "Collections of Vegetables" points must be given to the individual dishes which go to form the collection —*general uniformity* being considered only when other points are equal.

72. When "pointing" is necessary, the maximum points

allowed should vary with the relative value and importance of the different kinds, thus :—

	Points			Points
Artichokes, Globe . .	5	Kale	5
„ Jerusalem .	4	Leeks	6
Asparagus . . .	7	Lettuces . . .	5
Beans, Broad and Long-pod	6	Mushrooms . . .	7
		Onions	7
Beans, Runner & Kidney	7	Parsnips . . .	5
Beet	5	Peas	7
Broccoli . . .	7	Potatos . . .	7
Brussels Sprouts, plants	7	Radishes . . .	3
„ „ picked	5	Rhubarb . . .	4
Cabbage, Cooking .	5	Salsafy . . .	3
Cabbage, Red . .	5	Savoys . . .	5
Carrots . . .	5	Scorzonera . .	3
Cauliflower . . .	7	Seakale . . .	7
Celery	7	Spinach . . .	4
Cucumbers . . .	6	Tomatos . . .	7
Endive . . .	5	Turnips . . .	5
Eschallots . . .	3	Vegetable Marrows .	5

For other kinds *see* § 107.

73. *Note on the Cabbage (Brassica) Family.*—For exhibition purposes the following are considered to be distinct *kinds* of vegetables, viz. · Cauliflower, Brussels Sprouts, Cabbage, Borecole or Kale, Savoy. Cauliflower includes Broccoli, and for exhibition purposes is not distinct from it. § 3.

KINDS OF VEGETABLES.

74. *Artichokes, Globe.*—Of even size, rounded, scales well closed and fleshy.

Points 5 . Solidity 2
Size 1
Uniformity 1
Condition 1

75. *Artichokes, Jerusalem.*—Of uniform medium size, smooth, clear-skinned.

Points 4 : Uniformity 1
Smoothness 1
Clearness 1
Size 1

B

76. *Asparagus* —Of uniform length and thickness, scales well closed.

Points 7 : Condition 3
            Size 2
            Uniformity 2

77. *Beet.*—Of medium size, regular, evenly tapering ; length about 12 inches. Skin clear. Globular forms should be of medium uniform size, deep (not flat), with small tap-roots.

Points 5 : Quality of flesh 2
            Colour of flesh 1
            Uniformity 1
            Condition 1

78. *Broccoli.—See* Cauliflower.

79. *Beans, Broad and Long-pod.*—Pods of moderate and even size, well filled ; skins clear, and beans tender.

Points 6 : Size 2
            Uniformity 2
            Condition 2

80. *Beans, Runner and Dwarf Kidney.*—Pods long, straight, even, fleshy, brittle.

Points 7 : Size and form 2
            Fleshiness 2
            Condition 2
            Colour 1

81. *Brussels Sprouts—Plants.*—Stems straight, erect, densely covered with medium-sized firm sprouts.

Points 7 : Condition 2
            Cropping qualities . . . 2
            Size of sprouts 1
            Firmness 1
            Uniformity 1

Picked Sprouts.—Of medium size, firm, green.

Points 5 : Uniformity 2
            Size 1
            Firmness 1
            Condition 1

82. *Cabbages, cooking.*—Of medium size; hearts firm, well formed, tender.

Points 5 : Freshness 2
          Firmness 1
          Size 1
          Uniformity 1

Cabbages, red.—Of uniform size, firm, well coloured.

Points 5 : Firmness and colour . . . 3
          Size 1
          Uniformity 1

83. *Carrots.*—Of medium size according to variety, good form, skin and colour clear, bright; free from side-roots, flesh tender

Points 5 : Form and colour 2
          Size 1
          Condition 1
          Uniformity 1

84. *Cauliflower.*—Of medium size, firm, solid, rounded; free from stain and frothiness.

Points 7 : Purity and freshness . . . 3
          Size 2
          Solidity 2

85. *Celery.*—Heads and leaf-stalks solid; clean and well blanched.

Points 7 : Size 2
          Solidity 2
          Condition 2
          Uniformity 1

86. *Cucumbers.*—Straight, of uniform length, thickness, and colour; neck short; young, tender. May be either smooth or prickly.

Points 6 · Freshness, bloom, and crispness . 3
          Uniformity 2
          Size 1

87. *Eschallots.*—The old Cluster variety (*a*) should be shown in clusters as grown; the Russian, or red variety (*b*) should be shown in single bulbs.

(*a*) Points 3 : Uniformity of cluster . . 1
               Uniformity of cloves . . 1
               Size and firmness , . . 1

(*b*) Points 3 : Bright colour . . . 1
Size and firmness . . . 1
Shape and form . . . 1

88. *Endive.*—Hearts stout, well blanched, crisp and tender.
Points 5 : Size and stoutness . . . 2
Blanching 2
Uniformity 1

89. *Kale.*—Plants sturdy, stout in leafage, fresh, and of good size.
Points 5 . Size and freshness . . . 3
Stoutness of leaf 2

90. *Leeks.*—Stem long, thick, even, no tendency to bulbing ; skin clean and clear ; well blanched.
Points 6 : Size and length 2
Condition 2
Uniformity 2

91. *Lettuces, Cos and Cabbage.*—Hearts firm, well blanched, tender, unbroken.
Points 5 : Firmness and condition . . 2
Uniformity 2
Size 1

N.B.—Cos and Cabbage Lettuces should, as distinct Sections of Lettuce, have separate classes in Schedules.

92. *Mushrooms.*—Rounded ; edge unbroken ; gills deep pink or pinkish-brown, neither too pale nor too black.
Points 7 : Solidity 2
Condition 2
Uniformity 2
Size 1

93. *Onions.*—Skin clear, rounded or globular; the crown or neck small ; solid.
Points 7 : Size 2
Condition 2
Uniformity 2
Form 1

94. *Parsley* may be used for garnishing Vegetables, but does not in itself carry points. When exhibited for prizes it is included under Herbs.

95. *Parsnips.*—Of moderate length, well shouldered, evenly tapering; skin smooth.

Points 5 : Size 2
Smoothness and purity of skin . 2
Uniformity 1

96. *Peas.*—Pods large, well filled, of good colour, free from rust. Peas of fair size, fresh, and of good colour, quality, flavour, and appearance.

Points 7 : Condition and quality of pea . 3
Size of pod 2
Fulness of pod 2

97. *Potatos.*—Of medium size, free from disease; eyes few and shallow; skins clear; fresh.

Points 7 : Appearance and freedom from deep
or many eyes 3
Size 2
Uniformity 2

98. *Radishes.*—Of medium size, young, tender, and of bright colour.

Points 3 : Size 1
Condition 1
Uniformity 1

99. *Rhubarb.*—Stalks fresh and well coloured; straight, uniform, of medium size.

Points 4 : Size and uniformity . . . 2
Colour and freshness . . . 2

100. *Savoy.*—For points *see* Cabbage.

101 *Salsafy and Scorzonera.*—Large, clean, smooth, evenly tapering.

Points 3 · Size 1
Smoothness 1
Even form 1

102. *Seakale.*—Stout, clear, well blanched, not showing flower.

Points 7 . Size and solidity . . 3
Quality and purity . . 2
Uniformity 2

103. *Spinach.*—Leaves large, thick, fresh and green.

Points 4 : Substance . · . . . 2
Freshness 1
Colour 1

104. *Tomatos.*—Of medium size ; skins clear, unbroken ; flesh solid ; ripe.

Points 7 · Condition 3
        Size and appearance . . . 2
        Uniformity 2

105. *Turnips.*—Of medium size, with small tap-roots ; skin clear ; flesh crisp, juicy. May be of any colour externally—flesh white or yellow.

Points 5 : Solidity 2
        Uniformity 2
        Size 1

106. *Vegetable Marrows.*—Of medium size, about 1 foot in length ; fresh, tender ; of any colour.

Points 5 . Size and form 2
        Tenderness 2
        Uniformity 1

107. In the case of any Vegetables not enumerated above being shown, *e.g.*, Celeriac, Cardoons, Stachys, Witloof, Horseradish, small Saladings, Mustard, Cress, &c., not more than 3 points should be given.

108. *Herbs* should be shown in collections in neat bunches with clean, fresh, healthy leafage. The chief are Parsley, Sage, Thyme, Mint, Marjoram, Savory, Tarragon, and Fennel.

JUDGING SPECIMEN STOVE AND GREENHOUSE PLANTS.

109. When judging by points is necessary the following particulars should be carefully studied, making 8 points the maximum for single specimens .—

    (*a*) High-class cultivation . 4 points
    (*b*) Difficulty of culture . . . 2 ,,
    (*c*) Quality (irrespective of size) . 2 ,,

110. In plants grown specially for colouration of foliage, or where the colour of the foliage is material to the beauty of the plant (Caladiums, Crotons, &c.), two of the points allotted to Cultivation should be transferred to Colour.

111. In a class consisting of several plants, *variety* is very important, and, when not inconsistent with the Schedule, flowering plants (especially hard-wooded) should have more weight than foliage ones, as in most cases they are more difficult to produce.

The plants should all be pointed individually, and up to 4 more points may be added to the total, 2 for excellence in variety and 2 for arrangement of the specimens.

ORCHIDS.

112. Made-up plants should be absolutely discouraged.

A single specimen should have at least three times as many points as a pot, basket, or pan made up of several plants.

A new plant should not have extra points merely because it is new, but be judged on its merits.

Varieties involving special difficulty in cultivation should be specially considered.

VARIOUS PLANTS.

113. BEGONIA.

(a) Number, quality, and size of blooms in proportion to size of plant, 2 points.

(b) Distinctness and clearness of colour, 1 point.

(c) Abundance of healthy foliage, 2 points.

(d) Form of flower, 1 point.

(e) Erect flower-stems, 1 point.

114. CALCEOLARIA.

(a) Compactness of habit, with ample dark green foliage, 2 points.

(b) Flower-stems stout, carrying dense trusses just above the foliage, 2 points.

(c) Flowers regular in outline, well inflated, with a smooth surface, 2 points.

If selfs, the colour clear, distinct, and as nearly "solid" (uniform) as possible, 1 point.

115. CINERARIA.

(a) Habit moderately dwarf and compact, 2 points.

(b) Flowers large, petals broad and well rounded, 2 points.

(c) If selfs, the colour entire and unshaded; if edged flowers, half the petal white, forming a perfect zone, the disc dark, 2 points.

116. CYCLAMEN.

(*a*) Plants robust and sturdy, with ample bold, clean, fleshy leaves, 3 points.

(*b*) Flowers borne on stout stems above the foliage ; large, numerous, of good form, and clear in colour, 3 points.

117. FUCHSIA.

(*a*) Growth vigorous, free branching ; compact habit, 2 points.

(*b*) Quantity and quality of bloom, the sepals reflexing sufficiently to display the corolla, which should not be too widely expanded, 2 points.

(*c*) Foliage clean, fresh, and luxuriant, 1 point.

(*d*) Distinctness of colour, 1 point.

118. GLOXINIA.

Corolla circular, smooth on the edge ; lobes well rounded, overlapping each other, and perfectly flat ; throat widening upwards and in proportion to the length of the segments of the corolla. Stems stout. Colours clear and distinct. Foliage healthy, unbroken, of good substance, and covering the pot.

(*a*) Massive display of unblemished flowers, 2 points.

(*b*) Superior culture and unbroken foliage, 2 points.

(*c*) Freshness, quality and coloration of blooms, 2 points.

119. PELARGONIUM.

Show and Zonal.—Trained specimens should have a circular outline, and be well raised in the centre. Extreme flatness, obtrusively bent stems, small and unhealthy leaves, and small flower trusses are defects.

(*a*) Good form and ample foliage, 2 points.

(*b*) Trusses numerous, large and fully expanded, 2 points.

(*c*) Colours bright, clear, and distinct, 2 points.

120. *Ivy-leaved* specimens may be similarly trained, and also in free, pyramidal, or columnar form, for displaying their attractive characteristics.

(*a*) Good form and foliage, 2 points.

(*b*) Large, numerous, and fully expanded trusses, 2 points.

(*c*) Bright, clear, and distinct colours, 2 points.

121. Primula sinensis.

(a) Plants sturdy and vigorous; foliage stout, dark green, unbroken, and free from blemish, 2 points.

(b) Trusses large, supported above the foliage on strong stems, 2 points.

(c) Flowers large, circular, of good form and substance, with colours fresh and clear, 2 points.

Foliage Plants for Table Decoration.

122. *Table Plants* should be of moderate height, well-furnished, well balanced, of light and graceful habit, and of superior culture; very dense foliage being a defect. Pots should be relatively small, never exceeding six inches in diameter inside, and scrupulously clean.

Points 8. Cultivation and condition . . 3
Gracefulness . . . 3
Appropriate variety . . . 2

123. When Berried Plants are used they should be well furnished with an abundance of berries, which should be of a bright colour, and the foliage deep green.

Table Decorations.

124. No hard and fast rule can be laid down, as table decoration is so entirely a matter of individual taste, but the following are the lines on which judging should proceed:—

Points 20: Lightness and elegance . . . 8
Uniformity of colour, *or* ⎱
Harmonious blending ⎰ . . 6
Beauty of flowers and foliage . 6

When Fruit has to be taken into account, six more points may be added.

125. Hand Bouquets.

General Maxims.—Bouquets should not be so large as to be cumbersome, nor so small as to lack effect.

They should combine elegance in form and arrangement with suitability for the object in view; the stem being convenient in size and agreeable to the hand.

Rare flowers should not be favoured by Judges more than others of equal beauty and appropriateness. § 4.

Ferns, light foliage, or grasses must not be inserted *loosely* after the bouquet is made for hiding deficiencies and producing a mere temporary effect.

Wires and other mechanical aids must not be unduly exposed, or used so as to impart stiffness or formality.

The flowers must be neither faded nor closely packed, but free from blemish, and so associated that they all display their natural grace and beauty.

Points 20 : Size and general character appropriate for
         the purpose indicated in the Schedule .   .   5
         Fresh, well-chosen, unblemished flowers   .   .   5
         Pleasing association of flowers with ferns or
         other light and elegant foliage   .   .   .   5
         Colours in harmony with each other, and suitable
         for the object in view   5

N.B.—(i.) *Epergnes* and Vases; (ii.) *Button-holes*, and (iii.) *Sprays*, should be judged on the same principles, allowing up to 20 points for (i.) and 5 points each for (ii.) and (iii.).

Ferns or other garniture placed on the table as an *adjunct* to epergnes are to be removed by the Judges prior to adjudicating.

126. GROUPS OF PLANTS ARRANGED FOR EFFECT.

Object.—The pleasing arrangement of well-grown plants in the best possible condition of flowering and foliage.

Arrangement.—All the principal plants should be disposed so distinctly as to display their individual beauty. Originality in grouping, or in the association or contrast of plants, should be encouraged, when the effect is picturesque.

Defects.—Obtrusive pots, stakes or ties; overcrowding; packing to hide blemishes; inferior carpeting or other material; stereotyped form.

Points 20 · Elegance and beauty of arrange-
         ment   6
         Harmony in colour   .   .   .   5
         Quality and culture   .   .   .   5
         General finish   .   .   .   4

ROSES.

CUT BLOOMS.

127. The boxes in which Roses are exhibited should, as far as possible, be of the regulation size, viz 4 inches high in front and

18 inches wide, and be set out with moss or other suitable material. They should also be of a uniform length, viz. for 24 blooms, not less than 3 feet nor more than 3 feet 6 inches; for 12 blooms, not less than 1 foot 6 inches nor more than 2 feet; for 6 or 9 blooms, not less than 1 foot nor more than 1 foot 6 inches.

128. The showing of duplicate blooms, either under the same or different names, disqualifies the exhibit. Incorrect naming, if there be no duplicates, does not actually disqualify (§ 2).

The question of duplicates shall not be re-opened after the Judges have given their award.

129. The following Roses which are bracketed together are, for purposes of exhibition, considered synonymous, and are in every case to be treated as duplicates.—

Hybrid Perpetuals.

{ Charles Lefebvre
Marguerite Brassac
Paul Jamain

{ Comtesse de Choiseul
Marie Rady

{ Duke of Wellington
Rosieriste Jacobs

{ Eugénie Verdier
Marie Finger

{ Exposition de Brie
Ferdinand de Lesseps
Maurice Bernardin
Sir Garnet Wolseley

{ Grand Mogul
Jean Soupert

{ La Rosière
Prince C. de Rohan

{ Paul's Early Blush
Mrs. Harkness

Teas and Noisettes.

{ Alba Rosea
Josephine Malton
Madame Bravy
Madame de Sertot

{ Souvenir de S. A. Prince
The Queen

The climbing variety of any Rose cannot be shown in the same stand with it · for instance, Climbing Devoniensis cannot be shown in the same stand with Devoniensis.

130. All Roses must be exhibited as cut from the plants. With the exception of supports to keep the blooms erect, all artificial aid of any kind is strictly prohibited.

One point shall be deducted from any bloom "dressed" so as to alter its character. The use of added foliage disqualifies the stand unless specifically allowed by the Schedule.

131. Hybrid Teas must not be shown in the classes set apart

for Teas and Noisettes, but may be shown among Hybrid Perpetuals and in mixed classes.

132. A bloom or truss means the Rose as cut from the plant, with or without buds and foliage naturally pertaining.

133. *A Good Rose.*—The highest type of bloom is one which has form, size, brightness, substance, and good foliage, and which is, at the time of judging, in the most perfect phase of its possible beauty.

134. Form implies abundant petals of good substance, regularly and gracefully arranged within a circular outline, and having a well-formed centre.

135. Size implies that the bloom is a full-size representative specimen of the variety.

136. Brightness includes freshness, brilliancy, and purity of colour.

137. *A Bad Rose.*—The following are serious defects : faulty shape, confused or split centre, and faded colour ; being undersized, or oversized to the extent of coarseness.

138. Roses must be judged as they are in the boxes at the time of inspection.

139. In judging by points, 5 points should be given to an extraordinary specimen, 4 points for a very fine specimen, 3 points to an average high-class bloom, 2 points for a medium one, 1 point for one not so good, and no point at all for a bad bloom. A typical bloom of a 3-point Rose (which may be carried by one of the Judges) should be selected, and referred to from time to time, in order to keep up a uniform standard throughout the exhibits.

140. In the case of trebles (which must be arranged triangularly) each treble is to be regarded as a unit, and not as three separate blooms. Points must therefore be given as in Rule 139 —three points for an average high-class treble, two points for a medium treble, and so on.

141. In mixed classes the Teas and Noisettes must have no especial favour shown to them.

142. Where the blooms are found to be of equal merit, the judges should proceed to consider their general evenness, variety, arrangement, freshness, and setting up, the boxes being placed side by side, and in the same light for the purpose of comparison.

POT ROSES.

143. The Schedule should clearly define the size of the pots, quoting the inside measurement at the top.

144. The plants should be pyramidal or round, the blooms somewhat thrown up, the foliage down to the pot.

145. The flowers on all the plants should be as nearly as possible in the same stage of flowering.

146. The varieties should be of clear, decided, and varied colours.

147. The individual blooms should be large and fresh, borne on short-jointed, vigorous wood, with large and dark green foliage.

CHRYSANTHEMUMS.

148. All " points " are susceptible of division into four parts or " marks " when rendered necessary by very close competition.

CUT BLOOMS.

149. *Japanese Chrysanthemums* (*other than Anemones*).

Standard of Excellence.—(*a*) Diameter in proportion with depth ; (*b*) elegance of outline ; (*c*) brilliancy of colour, with freshness to the extremities of the florets.

Common Defects.—Coarseness accompanying size ; lack of fulness ; dulness and staleness.

Allotment of Points :
Points 8 : Diameter (relatively to the highest
potential of the variety), up to . 2
Depth 2
Fulness with symmetry . . 1
Colour 1
Freshness 1
Difficulty of cultivation . . 1

150. *Incurved* (*Chinese*) *Chrysanthemums.*

Standard of Excellence.—(*a*) Depth with breadth and firmness , (*b*) smoothness with symmetry ; (*c*) freshness with purity of colour and brightness.

Common Defects. — Breadth with flatness or looseness; roughness with angularity; staleness and dinginess.

Allotment of Points.

Points 8 · Depth with firmness .   .   . 2
General finish and symmetry   . 2
Diameter, up to 1
Colour 1
Freshness   1
Difficulty of cultivation   .   . 1

151. *Reflexed (Chinese) Chrysanthemums.*

Standard of Excellence. — (*a*) Size with symmetry; (*b*) freshness and brightness; (*c*) flat and perfectly imbricated florets.

Common Defects. — Florets curled at the edges or tips, and dulness of colour.

Allotment of Points :

Points 8 : Diameter, up to .   .   . 2
Depth 2
Colour 1
Freshness   1
Perfect imbrication   .   . 1
Flatness of floret   .   . 1

N.B. — In the case of a mixed class of Chinese and Japanese reflexed uniformity in length of florets in the Japanese section is not a necessary feature

152. *Anemone (Chinese) Chrysanthemums.*

Standard of Excellence. — (*a*) Cushion (disc florets) deep and symmetrical, (*b*) guard (ray) florets flat, broad, and equal in length; (*c*) colouration fresh and clear.

Common Defects. — Deformity of cushion; imperfect ray florets.

153. *Anemone (Japanese) Chrysanthemums.*

Standard of Excellence. — (*a*) Cushion prominent; (*b*) ray (guard) florets unequal in length and fresh to the tip.

Common Defects. — Deficiency of cushion; ray florets defective or shrunken.

Allotment of Points in the last two Sections.

Points 8 : Depth and breadth of cushion,
up to   3
Perfection of guard (ray) florets . 2
Clearness in colouration   .   . 2
Freshness   1

154. *Anemone Pompons.*

To be judged upon the same principles as ordinary Pompons.

155. *Pompons.*

Should be shown in bunches of three flowers, one on each stem, with their foliage, the back row being about 7 inches, the middle row 5½ inches, and the front row 4½ inches above the show board.

Standard of Excellence.—(a) Fulness with symmetry of outline; (b) brightness and clearness of colour; (c) foliage clean and healthy.

Common Defects.—Irregularity of outline and deficiency of colouration.

Allotment of Points ·

Points 8: Diameter, up to 2
Fulness 2
Clearness and brightness of colour 2
Foliage 1
General finish 1

156.—*Single Chrysanthemums.*

Standard of Excellence.—(a) Lightness with elegance of outline; (b) freshness and clearness of colour.

Common Defects.—Coarseness and excess of florets; florets incurving; staleness and dulness; confusion of disc.

Allotment of Points ·

Points 8: Diameter, up to 2
General finish and symmetry . 2
Colour 1
Firmness of florets . . . 1
Clearness and regularity of disc . 1
Freshness 1

N.B.—Three or more blooms of each variety in §§ 154, 155, 156 are to be regarded as one in allotting points.

157. *Trained Specimen Plants.*

Standard of Excellence.—Specimen plants should have the best possible blooms in combination with the best possible foliage displayed to the best possible advantage by skilful training. The training must not obliterate the natural character of the Chrysanthemum, and the bending of the stems (when necessary) ought to be done towards the base, not near the blooms. The depression or bending of the stems should be as obscure as possible, and the individual blooms supported on from six to twelve inches of well-foliaged straight stems , the shorter length of straight stem applying more especially to standards, and the longer to dwarf-trained plants.

Common Defects.—Obtrusive, bent, and tied-down stems ; blooms tied down close to framework.

Allotment of Points :

Points 16 · Number and quality of blooms
in proportion to size of plant,
up to   4
Abundance of healthy foliage   . 4
Excellence of training .   .   . 4
Freshness   4

158. *Conservatory (or Bush) Decorative Plants.*

Standard of Excellence.—These may be disbudded or not at the will of the cultivator, and may be cut down or not, and the stems should have perfect foliage to the base, and *must not be bent for dwarfing*, but may be supported by inconspicuous stakes. The natural habit of the Chrysanthemum must be retained, and the best cultural and decorative skill employed to obtain a well and naturally grown plant having the most imposing display of flowers.

Common Defects.—Bending and tying down stems for dwarfing; leafless stems and weak foliage; conspicuous stakes and ties.

Allotment of Points :

Points 16 . Display of bloom, up to   .   . 4
Healthy foliage down to the pot . 4
Freshness   4
Inconspicuousness of supports   . 4

159. *Groups arranged for Effect.*

Standard of Excellence.—THE MOST PLEASING ARRANGEMENT OF WELL-GROWN PLANTS SHOULD BE THE MAIN OBJECT IN VIEW. The plants best adapted to the purpose are those which represent (*a*) the most perfect health and foliage, with (*b*) the most attractive blooms, and (*c*) effective association of colours. Freedom of arrangement with diversity, displaying the merits of the plant individually as well as collectively, is most desirable. Boldness and originality of design, if the effect be picturesque, should be considered of importance in judging this class.

Common Defects.—Obtrusive pots, stakes, and stems; crowding for a "face" of colour.

Allotment of Points:

Points 20: Freedom of arrangement with
diversity, up to . . . 8
Perfect health and leafage . . 6
Harmony of colours . . 3
Quality of blooms . . 3

This allotment of points must be adhered to whether foliage or other plants are by the Schedule permitted to be added or not.

N.B.—Schedule-makers should state clearly either—(1.) No other plants (foliage or otherwise) may be added; or (ii.) Foliage plants may be added; or (iii.) Foliage and other plants may be added; or (iv.) Chrysanthemums only may be used *in the group,* but an edging of foliage plants may be added.

HARDY PLANTS AND FLOWERS.

160. *Annuals* are plants which, naturally, begin and end their growth, and ripen seed, and die, within twelve months.

161. *Biennials* are plants ordinarily requiring two full seasons to complete their life-growth, and which, as a rule, die before the third season—*e.g.*, Foxglove, Sweet William, Honesty, &c.

162. *Perennials* are plants of many years' continuance.

163. *Herbaceous,* are plants with stems which die down yearly, but having rootstocks remaining alive throughout the winter. For garden purposes the word "rootstock" includes all bulbs, corms, and tubers.

164. *Suffruticose* are plants of more or less shrubby growth, and tufted evergreens whose stems do not die down in winter.

165. A class in a Schedule entitled "Hardy Perennials" would exclude 160 and 161, but would embrace all the rest, including such as Rose, Genista, Clematis, Syringa, and others of a similar nature, which come in under 164; in fact, every imaginable hardy garden flower except 160 and 161.

A class entitled "Hardy Herbaceous" would exclude 160, 161, and 164.

c

It is strongly recommended that in the framing of Schedules the simple words **Hardy Flowers** should be adopted. This would include every imaginable hardy flower.

If, however, it is desired to limit the class to what are ordinarily called "Perennials," this may be done by adding " *excluding annuals and biennials.*"

If it is further wished to exclude the flowers of shrubs (and trees), as the Moutan Pæony, Cistus, Helianthemum, Fuchsia, Syringa, &c., add " *excluding annuals, biennials, shrubby plants, and trees.*"

166. If, contrary to the above advice, a prize be offered for *Hardy Herbaceous Plants*, the Schedule should say distinctly " *excluding Lilies and other bulbs, corms, and tubers,*" if it is *desired* to exclude them ; and if such words are not added, it must be understood that bulbs, corms, and tubers are, for garden purposes, included in the term "Herbaceous plants."

167. If the word " Perennial " is used it must be distinctly understood to exclude such plants as the common Foxglove, Honesty, Sweet William, and all others which are, as a rule, raised from seed annually, and grown as biennials only.

168. Every specimen in Hardy Flower classes must be shown in bunches cut from plants which have been actually growing in the open border, and (except in the case of Annuals) *through the last winter* at least. The number of spikes or trusses must vary with the varieties shown.

169. In order to regulate the maximum size of the bunches, Schedules should restrict the diameter (inside measurement) of the tubes, or other vessels, in which the flowers may be shown, and insist that all the stems shall reach the water—*e.g.* :

Class ——. *Twelve bunches of Hardy Flowers, distinct kinds* [or *distinct varieties*]; *inside of tubes, &c., not to exceed 3 inches diameter at the top, and* **all the stems to reach the water.**

It is obvious that in order to make the exhibit symmetrical the 3-inch tubes would only be used for the largest flowers in the back row, as Pæonies, Delphiniums, &c., and smaller tubes for the smaller flowers in front. It is necessary to insist that the stalks of all the flowers reach the water, in order to guard against the building-up of bunches.

170. The word " *distinct* " should never be used in Schedules in connection with Hardy Flower classes without

the addition of the word " kinds " or of the word " varieties "—
thus·

*Twelve bunches of Hardy Flowers, distinct "kinds": or
distinct "varieties."*

171. If the word "kinds" is used, only one representative
of any genus or family may be included—*i.e.* one bunch of one
Poppy, one bunch of one Delphinium, one bunch of one Pæony,
and so on. Two bunches of Poppies (say one of Nudicaule
and another of Orientale) would disqualify.

172. And further, if the word "kinds" is used, the mixture
of colour variations in the bunches *must* always disqualify.

173. If the word "varieties" is used, two or more of the
12 items may lawfully consist of distinct varieties of the same
genus—*e.g.*, they may all 12 be distinct varieties of Delphinium
hybridum, or, say, 4 Delphinium hybridum vars., 6 Phlox
decussata vars., and 2 Helianthus rigidus vars., or any other
similar arrangement, provided only that the *varieties* are distinct
in themselves.

174. And further, if the words " distinct varieties " stand
alone, the mixture of colour variations in the bunches *must*
always disqualify.

175. If it is desired to allow the mixture of colour variations
in the bunches (*e.g.* white, yellow, and orange Iceland Poppies
light and dark blue Delphiniums, crimson and white Phloxes,
and so on), the Schedule should state the fact expressly, thus :

*Class ——. Twelve bunches of Hardy Flowers, distinct
varieties, colour variations in the bunches allowed, inside
diameter of tubes, &c., not to exceed 3 inches at the top, and all
the stems to reach the water.* § 169.

176. Florists' flowers, if hardy, may be shown under the
general title of Hardy Flowers.

177. The points to look for in a stand of Hardy Flowers
are :—

	Points	
Quality of blooms . .	3	⎫
Freshness . . .	2	⎬ Apply to each bunch.
Elegance of habit . . .	2	
Rarity or difficulty of cultivation	3	⎭
Variety of form and colour .	2	⎫ Apply to the exhibit as
Arrangement, naming, &c. .	2	⎭ a whole.

VARIOUS FLOWERS.

Section I.

178. AURICULA, SHOW.

The truss to consist of not less than five fully developed flowers for exhibition purposes.   Points 10.

(*a*) The corolla round, smooth on the edge, perfectly flat, 2 points.

(*b*) The tube yellow or lemon, round, filled with the anthers, hiding the stigma from view, 1 point.

(*c*) Paste smooth, solid, pure white, 2 points.

(*d*) Ground colour dense, forming a perfect circle next the paste, 2 points

(*e*) The edge green, grey-white, or unshaded self colour, 2 points.

(*f*) The stem strong and sufficiently long to bear the truss above the foliage, 1 point.

179. AURICULA, ALPINE.

Points 6.

(*a*) A well-formed flat pip, 2 points.

(*b*) Tube filled with the anthers, 1 point.

(*c*) Centre yellow, cream, or white, destitute of farina, 1 point.

(*d*) The edge a zone of some dark colour, shaded to a paler tint, 2 points.

180. CARNATION AND PICOTEE.

Points 6.

(*a*) The flower not less than two and a half inches in diameter, consisting of a number of well-formed petals, neither so many as to give it a crowded appearance, nor so few as to make it appear thin, 1 point.

(*b*) Petals broad and stiff, the outer ones well rounded, 2 points.

(*c*) Ground white, flakes of colour clear and distinct; the fewer spots the better, 1 point.

(*d*) The calyx should be long, and not burst while the flower is opening, 2 points.

Picotees the same size as to petals and ground as the Carnations, edge of petal smooth and well rounded; the colour uniformly disposed on the margin, light or heavy.

The yellow-ground Carnations or Picotees are subject to the same rules as the white-ground. The selfs should be large and well formed.

181. DAHLIA.

Show and Fancy.—The blooms should be of good size, with even, rounded outline; the petals (or florets) rounded or fluted, of a shell shape; centre of bloom well up and even, but close and not over-developed. Colour bright and fresh. The back petals not faded.

Points 7: Form 2
    Good centre. . . . 2
    Colour and freshness . . . 2
    Size 1

Pompon Dahlias.—Should be shown in bunches well displayed. Flowers relatively small, yet very dense of petal, rounded and having good centres. They should be miniature forms of Show-Dahlias.

Points 7: Attractive setting-up . . 2
    Form of flower . . . 2
    Colour and freshness . . . 2
    Good centres 1

Cactus Dahlias.—If shown in bunches they should be effectively displayed. Flowers of medium size, the florets long, twisted or pointed, evenly set; centre moderately developed, but without a green tinge. Flowers should have long stalks.

Points 7: Effective setting-up . . . 2
    Colour and freshness . . . 2
    Form and size 2
    Good centre 1

Single Dahlias.—Should be shown in bunches, and effectively displayed. Flowers of medium size. Good rounded form, flat, broad petals of good substance. Colours clear, and in bicolors clearly defined.

Points 7: Effective arrangement . . 2
    Colour and freshness . . . 2
    Form 2
    Size 1

182. GLADIOLUS.

(*a*) Form, with size, substance, and freshness, 2 points.
(*b*) Length and symmetry of spike, on which the flowers

should all face to the front, and at such distances as just to hide the stem, 3 points.

(c) Colours rich and bright in dark varieties, and clear and soft in light varieties, 1 point.

Defects. — Winged spikes, where the flowers are placed opposite to each other, showing a naked stalk in front. Bleached and faded colours through over-shading in boxes Short crowded spikes and flowers, with narrow segments, as seen in Saundersii types.

183. HOLLYHOCK.

(a) Spike stout and covered with flowers nearly touching each other, 2 points.

(l) Flowers fresh, full, high centre, smooth outline, free from pockets, 2 points.

(c) Guard petals, about half an inch beyond the centre ; smooth, flat, and circular, 1 point.

(d) If self, clear and decided , if shaded or mottled, pleasing and harmonious, 1 point.

184. PÆONY.

(a) Size and fulness of bloom, 2 points.

(b) Regularity of guard petals, 1 point.

(c) Compactness and symmetry, 1 point.

(d) Clearness of colour and freshness, 1 point.

(e) Average evenness of blooms, 1 point.

185. PANSY, SHOW (BELTED OR MARGINED BLOOMS).

(a) Form of flower circular, and smoothness of petal and edge, 1 point.

(b) Stoutness and finish of texture, 1 point.

(c) Clearness of ground colour, 1 point.

(d) Denseness and solidity of blotch, 1 point.

(e) Similarity of tint, evenness and regularity of belting, 1 point.

(f) Brilliancy and freshness, 1 point.

186. PANSY, SHOW (SELF BLOOMS).

(a) Texture and smoothness of petal, 2 points.

(b) Uniformity of colour, $1\frac{1}{2}$ points.

(c) White brows in a dark self, 1 point.

(d) Brilliancy and freshness, $1\frac{1}{2}$ points.

187. Pansy, Fancy (Show Blooms).

(a) Circularity, smoothness of petal and edge, 1½ points.

(b) Texture thick, velvety, flat, ½ point.

(c) Harmonious colours without confusion, ½ point.

(d) Blotch dense, large, regular, 1 point.

(e) Size combined with other qualities, 1½ points.

(f) Brilliancy and freshness, 1 point.

188. Viola.

(a) Good outline and stoutness of petal, 1 point.

(b) Smoothness of petal and edge, 1 point.

(c) In selfs, well-defined colours, 1 point.

(d) In belted and blotched flowers, harmony without confusion, 2 points.

(e) Erect stout stems, blooms facing well to the front, 1 point.

189. Pentstemon.

(a) Spikes stout, long, full of flower on one side, slightly drooping, 2 points.

(b) Flowers expanded, with the lobes well rounded, and forming a circular outline, stout and firm in substance, 2 points.

(c) Colours bright, clear, and well defined, 1 point.

Painted or striped throats should have the markings distinct.

190. Phlox.

(a) Spikes full, dense, and symmetrical, 2 points.

(b) Flowers flat, circular in outline, stout in texture, and fresh, 8 points.

(c) Colours clear and decided, 1 point.

(d) Stout, erect stem, 1 point.

191. Pinks as cut Show Blooms.

(a) Petals thick, broad, smooth on the edge, 1½ points.

(b) Pure white ground, dense even lacing, 1½ points.

(c) Well-defined narrow margin of white to petals, 1 point.

(d) Well-placed petals, forming a full half ball, 1½ points.

(e) Brightness and freshness, ½ point.

192. Polyanthus, Gold-laced.

(*a*) Strong straight stem, 4 to 6 inches in length, $\frac{1}{2}$ point.

(*b*) Footstalks of pips just long enough to bring all together in a compact symmetrical whole, $\frac{1}{2}$ point.

(*c*) A truss of not less than five well-expanded flowers, 1 point.

(*d*) The centre pure, without stain, and uniform with that on the edges, $1\frac{1}{2}$ points.

(*e*) The lacing thinly and regularly laid on round each segment, cutting down to the centre, $1\frac{1}{2}$ points.

(*f*) The ground colour red or black, unshaded, and dense, 1 point

193. Polyanthus, Fancy.

(*a*) Strong, stout, erect flower-stems, 1 point.

(*b*) Compactly arranged heads of bloom, 2 points.

(*c*) Large, stout, finely formed pips, having thrum eyes, 2 points.

(*d*) Brilliancy and freshness, 1 point.

N.B.—Fancy Polyanthuses must not be judged as the Gold-laced are.

194. Primrose (P. acaulis).

(*a*) Habit of growth, tufted and compact, 2 points.

(*b*) Flowers solitary, freely produced, on long peduncles, forming a symmetrical mass, regularly displayed, 2 points.

(*c*) Flowers thrum-eyed, stout, circular; colours clear and distinct, with the absence of stains in the centre, 2 points.

195. Pyrethrum.

(*a*) Flowers imbricated, forming half a ball; the florets laid numerously and regularly, decreasing in size as they reach the top and filling up the centre, 2 points.

(*b*) The ray florets sufficiently displayed, forming a neat base to the flower, 2 points.

(*c*) The colours clear and bright when deep, pure and pleasing when pale, 2 points.

Single.—To possess one or two rows of ray florets in symmetrical arrangement, and a clear bright yellow disc, 2 points.

196. TULIP (LATE FLORISTS', BROKEN OR RECTIFIED).

(a) Flowers with six petals only, broad, smooth on the edge, level on the top, and bending upward from the base to form a good shoulder, 2 points.

(b) The base pure yellow in the case of the Bizarre, and pure white in the case of the Byblœmen and the Rose, the stamens free from any stain, 2 points.

(c) A feathered flower to have the colours laid on in harmonious pencillings round the edge only of the petal, the feathering not to break off anywhere round the edge before finishing at the base, 2 points.

(d) The flame should form a bold beam of colour up the petal centre, throwing out sharp tongues striking into the pencillings of the feathered edge, 2 points.

Breeders, 6 points. The class or basal colour should be clear yellow in the Bizarre, and clear white in the Byblœmen and the Rose. Bizarres have reddish and yellowish brown, dull red, and something approaching mahogany on their petals. Byblœmens have lilac or slate-coloured petals; some soft; others dark in tint. Roses have pink, rose, red. or scarlet petals.

197. VARIOUS FLOWERS.

Section II.

Antirrhinum	Narcissus
Aster	Phlox Drummondi
Delphinium	Stocks
Gaillardia	Sweet Peas
Hyacinth	Sweet William
Iris	Tulips, Forced
Lily of the Valley	Zinnia
Michaelmas Daisy	&c. &c. &c.

If prizes are offered for any of the above, Judges must take into consideration their (a) cultivation, (b) form, (c) freshness and (d) colour, allotting points on the following general lines :—

Culture	.	.	3 points.
Form	.	.	2 ,,
Freshness	.	.	2 ,,
Colour	.	.	1 ,,

SUGGESTIONS TO EXHIBITORS.

1. Note very carefully and observe strictly the conditions in the Schedule as to the time named for the Judges to commence their duties.

2. Comply exactly with the specified number of fruits and vegetables for a dish, or flowers for a stand; also the number of dishes of fruits and vegetables, or bunches of flowers, for a collection, as the case may be.

3. Bear distinctly in mind that one item more or less disqualifies, also that no Judge has the right to himself rectify the errors of a competitor, and thus "assist" him to win a prize. § 7.   But Judges, when they think fit to do so, may draw official attention to irresponsible errors.   §§ 7A and 7B.

4. Be most careful in seeing that each card is placed with the particular exhibit to which it applies, and not, by accident, to another.

5. Read carefully all sections in the foregoing Rules which in any way relate to your proposed exhibit, and if in any difficulty of understanding the same write to the Secretary of your Society or Show.

6. It should be remembered that shortcomings in some of the matters above indicated have led in the past, and must lead in the future, to delay and disappointment; also it should be fully recognised that half-an-hour's delay in completing the arrangements is so much time taken from the Judges, who thus have to discharge their duties hurriedly, this of necessity increasing the possibility of mistakes, which ought by every available means to be avoided.

7. Though the responsibility of having all arrangements completed in accordance with the Rules and Regulations rests with the managers of shows, yet exhibitors may and should help materially in carrying them out to the mutual advantage of all.

APPENDIX A.

POINT-JUDGING.

Point-judging is the most exact of all systems of judging, and in very close competitions it is sometimes impossible to demonstrate the correctness of a decision without giving a numerical value to every point of merit discovered in the several items of an exhibit.

In some Schedules it is announced that certain specially important classes will be judged by this system, and that the points allotted to each item will be exposed to public view. There is then no occasion to ask why A is placed before B, or B before C, the reason being apparent by the marks recorded for each item of each exhibit, and the relative position of each competitor is seen by the sum total of the addition of the marks. The exposure of the detailed points is found to be very educational to the general public. Unless the exposure of the points is expressly stipulated, it is not *necessary* to display more than the sum total. The course to be pursued must in this respect be decided in each case by the authorities of the Show.

In classes in which point-judging is not stipulated, it is not necessary to resort to the practice except in *close* contests, but in every case of doubt, or when the Judges cannot give an unhesitating and unanimous decision, point-judging is the surest, safest, and in the end generally the quickest way of overcoming the difficulty.

As a corollary of this system it seems at first sight as if the prize money should be divided in proportion to the number of marks obtained by each competitor, but this does not necessarily follow ; some considering that the value of each point *above* a certain average should be greater than the value of each point *below* it, because the excellence and skill needed to score *the winning point* or points is well worth the usual difference between first and second prizes. Unquestionably the difficulty of scoring one more point increases as the maximum procurable is approached. If, for example, ten points are the maximum, it is easy to obtain the first three or four, but comparatively difficult to advance from the eighth to the ninth, and still more so to score the tenth.

The system of point-value does not, therefore, *necessarily* follow on the adoption of point-judging. The two are quite distinct, and whilst the system of point-judging cannot be too strongly recommended in all close contests, the system of point-value requires consideration, and should not be adopted too hastily.

POINT-VALUE.

Point-value is the system whereby, instead of a definite sum being announced beforehand in the Schedule for the first prize and another lesser sum for the second, and so on, a lump sum is, instead, allotted to a class, to be divided into two, three, four, or more prizes, as may be announced in the Schedule, in proportion to the number of points obtained by the respective competitors.

It is therefore evident that, though point-judging does not necessitate point-value, point-value can only be carried out after point-judging.

Point-judging is obviously the work of the Judges; point-value is entirely the work of the officials of the Show.

When prizes are announced in the Schedule to be awarded according to the system of point-value, the Judges having handed to the Secretary (on sheets provided for the purpose) a record of the number of points they adjudge to each competitor in the class, the Secretary divides the sum set apart for that class between them as follows* :—

Supposing that it is stated in the schedule that the number of prizes to be awarded in the class is four†, then the number of points scored by the four leading competitors are added together, and the sum set apart for the prizes having first been reduced to shillings, pence, and farthings (if necessary) is divided by the total number of points. This gives the value of each point, and the multiplication of this point-value by the number of points each of the four leading

* The following rule is taken in substance from a Paper by Mr. John Wright, F.R.H.S., V.M.H., in the Journal of the Royal Horticultural Society, Vol. xxi. p. 517, which consult upon the whole subject.

† The rule holds good for any other number which may be specified in the Schedule

competitors has obtained, gives his individual share of the sum total set apart in the Schedule for the prizes in that class. In other words :—

Supposing

Four prizes are announced in the Schedule, and £5 are set apart for them ,

and supposing

A gets 86 points.
B ,, 78 ,,
C ,, 65 ,,
D ,, 62 ,,

Add the points together 86 + 78 + 65 + 62 = 291.
Reduce £5 to farthings = 4,800 farthings.
Divide 4,800 by 291 = $16\frac{144}{291}$, say $16\frac{1}{2}$.

Therefore the point-value is $16\frac{1}{2}$ farthings for each point scored.

Thus A with 86 points gets $86 \times 16\frac{1}{2}$ = £1 9 6
     B ,, 78 ,,   ,, $78 \times 16\frac{1}{2}$ = £1 6 8
     C ,, 65 ,,   ,, $65 \times 16\frac{1}{2}$ = £1 2 8
     D ,, 62 ,,   ,, $62 \times 16\frac{1}{2}$ = £1 1 2

Total . 291   £5 0 0

Under the ordinary system the probability is the £5 would have been divided thus :—

A first   prize £2 0 0
B second   ,,   £1 10 0
C third   ,,   £1 0 0
D fourth   ,,   £0 10 0

Thus in the case supposed above the exhibit judged first would take 10s. 6d. less by the point-value system, and the exhibit judged fourth would obtain 10s. 6d. more than under the ordinary system.

It should also be borne in mind that sometimes only a single point, or even half a point, divides first from second or second from third, and then it is that the disparity in the amounts of the prizes under the old system seems to some so unjust.

The officials of a Show should consider well and carefully whether it is or is not expedient for the good of Horticulture to adopt the point-value system for the leading class or classes of their Schedule.

For the purpose of point-judging, a sheet should be provided for *each* exhibit, these sheets having down the left-hand side the names of every eligible fruit (or other product) in mixed "collections," then following in columns the number of staged dishes of each kind to be pointed, the maximum number of marks allowed for each dish, a blank column for the awards of the judges, and a final column for remarks.

An example of a Decorated Dessert Table Sheet, as used at Shrewsbury, will make the matter clear:—

Sixteen dishes of Fruits to be selected from the following	•Dishes	Possible No. of points	Points awarded	Remarks
Apples .	1	7		
"	2	7		
Apricots .	1	6		
"	2	6		
Cherries	1	5		
Figs . .	1	7		
" . .	2	7		
Grapes, black	1	9		
" "	2	9		
" Muscats, white	1	10		
" any other white	2	9		
Melon . . .	1	8		
"	2	8		
Nectarines	1	8		
"	2	8		
Peaches .	1	8		
" .	2	8		
Pears . .	1	8		
" . .	2	8		
Plums	1	8		
" . .	2	8		
Pine	1	10		
Strawberries . . .	1	6		
Beauty of flowers and foliage .	—	8		
Harmonious blending of colour .	—	10		
General arrangement for effect .	—	10		

* The figures 1 and 2 in this column simply denote No. 1 dish and No. 2 dish of those Fruits, of which, in this class at Shrewsbury, exhibitors were allowed to show duplicates if they liked. It is imperative that each and every dish be pointed and the points entered separately for each and every dish, and not lumped together. *See* § 50.

APPENDIX B.

APPLES, PEARS, AND PLUMS.

(a) *for Dessert*, (b) *for Cooking*.

With a view to removing difficulties and resolving doubts as to the distinction to be drawn between Dessert and Kitchen Apples, Pears, and Plums, the Council of the Royal Horticultural Society have caused the following lists to be prepared for the guidance of their Judges at the Society's exhibitions and shows.

The Council fully recognise that the line of separation between Dessert and Kitchen Fruits must be entirely arbitrary, and to a great extent a matter of taste—which differs widely. They do not, therefore, wish it to be supposed that the varieties named in the one list are unfit for use in the other. Everyone is at liberty to use a variety for any purpose he likes, but in their opinion a fixed line of division between the two classes, **for Exhibition purposes,** is absolutely necessary to secure uniformity, and avoid confusion and disappointment at their shows. The lists are obviously not necessarily binding on any other societies.

The Council are also fully aware that some varieties of beautiful appearance, which do not in their opinion come up to **Dessert Standard** as regards flavour, are often placed on the dessert table. Everyone is at liberty to ornament their tables with brightly-coloured fruits as well as with beautiful flowers; but beauty in fruits, although a great additional advantage when it accompanies flavour and quality, does not, when standing alone, entitle a variety to rank in the technical exhibition sense as a Dessert Fruit.

It would be impossible to draw up lists to which everyone would agree as to the position assigned to each individual variety, and it is only by mutual concessions that a general working agreement can be reached, but that it is a good thing to endeavour to bring about such agreement the Council have no doubt whatever.

The following list will be found to include the great majority of varieties at present shown for exhibition. In the case of those not named herein the Judges must decide for themselves in which class they will put them, always bearing in mind the principles expressed in the preceding paragraphs. Judges are requested in the case of any variety of sterling merit, omitted here, coming to their notice, to notify their action to the Secretary of the Royal Horticultural Society with a view to future revision of the lists.

The object of the following lists should be borne in mind. It is only to decide between Dessert and Cooking varieties. It is in no sense to recommend any, much less all those mentioned, as being desirable varieties to plant. Such advice must be sought elsewhere and not here.

The nomenclature follows the Fifth Edition, 1884, of the late Dr. Hogg's Fruit Manual.

APPLES.

DESSERT.	COOKING.
Adam's Pearmain.	Albury Park Nonesuch.
Akera, or Okera.	Alfriston.
Allen's Everlasting.	Annie Elizabeth.
Allington Pippin	Beauty of Kent.
American Mother.	Beauty of Stoke.
Ashmead's Kernel.	Bedfordshire Foundling.
Baumann's Winter Reinette.	Belle de Pontoise.
Beauty of Bath.	Bess Pool.
Benoni.	Betty Geeson.
Blenheim Pippin.	Bietigheimer Red.
Blue Pearmain.	Bismarck.
Boston Russet.	Bowhill Pippin.
Braddick's Nonpareil	Bramley's Seedling.
Brownlees' Russet.	Byford Wonder.
Calville Rouge Précoce.	Castle Major.
Cardinal, or Peter the Great.	Cellini.
Claygate Pearmain.	Chelmsford Wonder.
Cobham.	Cox's Pomona.
Cockle's Pippin.	Domino.
Cornish Aromatic.	Duchess of Oldenburg.
Cornish Gilliflower.	Dumelow's Seedling Welling-
Court Pendu Plat.	ton, or Normanton Wonder.
Court of Wick.	Dutch Codlin.
Cox's Orange.	Early Julyan.

APPLES—*continued.*

DESSERT.	COOKING.
D'Arcy Spice.	Early Rivers.
Devonshire Quarrenden.	Ecklinville.
Duchess' Favourite.	White Transparent.
Duke of Devonshire.	Emperor Alexander.
Dutch Mignonne.	Forester
Early Peach.	Frogmore Prolific.
Egremont Russet.	Galloway Pippin.
Fearn's Pippin.	Gloria Mundi.
Gascoyne's Scarlet.	Gold Medal, or Crystal Palace.
Golden Reinette.	Golden Noble.
Gravenstein.	Golden Spire.
Herefordshire Pearmain.	Gooseberry.
Hubbard's Pearmain.	Gospatric.
Irish Peach.	Grantonian.
James Grieve.	Greenup's Pippin, Yorkshire Beauty, or Counsellor.
Joaneting.	Grenadier
Keddleston Pippin	Hambledon Deux Ans.
Kentish Pippin, or Colonel Vaughan's.	Hambling's Seedling.
Kerry Pippin.	Hoary Morning.
King Harry.	Hormead Pearmain.
King of Tomkins County.	Hawthornden, New.
King of the Pippins.	Hollandbury.
Lady Sudeley.	Keswick Codlin.
Lord Burghley.	Lady Henniker.
Lord Hindlip.	Lane's Prince Albert.
Mabbott's Pearmain.	Lord Derby.
Mannington's Pearmain.	Lord Grosvenor.
Margaret, or Red Juneating.	Lord Suffield.
Margil.	Maltster.
May Queen.	Manks Codlin.
Melon Apple.	Mère de Ménage.
Mr. Gladstone	Mrs. Barron.
Northern Spy.	Newton Wonder.
Old Nonpareil.	New Northern Greening.
Oslin.	Northern Dumpling.
Red Astrachan.	Peasgood's Nonesuch.
Reinette de Canada.	Potts' Seedling.

D

APPLES—*continued.*

DESSERT	COOKING.
Ribston Pippin.	Rivers' Codlin.
Rosemary Russet.	Royal Jubilee.
Ross Nonpareil.	Rymer.
Roundway Magnum Bonum	Sandringham.
Scarlet Nonpareil.	Sanspareil.
September Beauty.	Schoolmaster.
Sturmer Pippin.	Seaton House.
St. Edmund's Pippin	Small's Admirable.
Washington	Spencer's Favourite, or Queen Caroline.
Wealthy.	Stirling Castle.
Williams' Favourite	Stone's, or Loddington.
Worcester Pearmain.	Striped Beefing.
Wyken Pippin.	The Queen.
Yellow Ingestrie.	Tibbett's Pearmain.
	Tower of Glammis.
	Twenty Ounce.
	Tyler's Kernel.
	Wadhurst Pippin.
	Wagener.
	Waltham Abbey Seedling.
	Warner's King.
	Winter Quoining, or Queening.

PEARS.

It will be sufficient to say that the following do not rank for exhibition as Dessert Pears at the Society's shows :—

Bellissime d'Hiver.	Grosse Calebasse.
Beurré Clairgeau.	Idaho.
Black Worcester	King Edward.
Catillac.	Morel.
Directeur Alphand.	Poire d'Auch.
Duchesse de Mouchy.	Summer Compôte.
Gilogil	Triomphe de Jodgoine.
	Uvedale's St. Germain.
	Verulam.
	Vicar of Winkfield.

PLUMS.

All Plums can, if not otherwise required, be advantageously used for cooking, especially if they are not fully ripe, but this does not constitute them Cooking varieties in the technical exhibition sense. Similarly, some Cooking Plums, *e.g.*, Blue Impératrice, if left to hang on the tree until they are shrivelled, become fit for dessert, as far as flavour is concerned, but this does not render them Dessert varieties from an exhibition point of view.

DESSERT.	COOKING.
Angelina Burdett.	Archduke.
Anna Spath.	Automne Compôte.
Boulouf.	Belgian Purple.
Coe's Golden Drop.	Belle de Louvain.
Coe's Violet.	Belle de Septembre.
De Montfort.	Curlew.
Denniston's Superb.	Cox's Emperor.
Early Favourite.	Diamond.
Gages, all varieties.	Duke of Edinburgh.
Golden Esperen.	Early Normandy.
Ickworth Impératrice.	Early Prolific.
Impérial de Milan.	Gisborne's.
Jefferson	Goliath.
Kirke's.	Grand Duke.
Oullins Golden.	Heron.
Précoce de Tours.	Impératrice, Blue and White
Purple Gages, all varieties.	Magnum Bonum, Red and White.
Reine Claude, all varieties.	Mitchelson's.
St. Etienne.	Monarch.
Transparent, all varieties.	Orleans, all varieties.
Washington.	Pershore.
	Pond's Seedling.
	Prince Engelbert
	Prince of Wales.
	Sultan.
	The Czar.
	Victoria.
	Wyedale.

SPECIMEN OF CLASS CARD : FACE.

ROYAL HORTICULTURAL SOCIETY,

Established A.D. 1804.   Incorporated A.D. 1809.

117 VICTORIA STREET, WESTMINSTER, S.W.

Class ....

Description to be written here ....

Exhibitor's Name and Address ....

Gardener (if any) Mr. ....

At the top of this Card one of the Judges should attach a gummed label bearing the words "First Prize," "Second Prize," &c., as the case may be.

SPECIMEN OF CLASS CARD : BACK.

CLASS.

Entry No.

Prize.

[Copies of this Card (with the Name and Address blank) may be obtained from 117 Victoria Street, Westminster. It is kept in stock on White, Yellow, Pink and Blue cards of regulation size, and is sold in packets of not less than 50 of one colour. Price per 50, free by post, 2s. 6d. prepaid. If no colour is stated, White will be sent. § 27.]

The Judges should write in words "First," "Second," or "Third," as the case may be, in front of the word "Prize" above, as a check to the gummed label on the Face side.

APPENDIX D.

SPECIMEN OF JUDGE'S CARD.

(Name of Society or Show.)

Date... 18 .

CLASSES .... TO .... INCLUSIVE.

JUDGES...

Class	1st Prize	2nd Prize	3rd Prize	4th	REMARKS
		Entry Number on Class Card			
1					
2					
3					
4					
5					
6					
7					
8					
9					
10					
11					
12					
13					
14					
15					
16					

55

Class	1st Prize	2nd Prize	3rd Prize	4th	REMARKS
		Entry Number on Class Card			
17					
18					
19					
20					
21					
22					
23					
24					
25					
26					
27					
28					
29					
30					
31					
32					
33					
34					
35					
36					
37					
38					
39					
40					
41					
42					
43					
44					
45					
46					
47					
48					
49					
50					

[Copies of this Card may be obtained from 117 Victoria Street, Westminster. It is kept in stock printed on thick white cardboard, and is sold in packets of not less than 10. Price per 10, free by post, 1s. 3d. prepaid. § 27.]

Hon. Sec.

AFFILIATION
OF
LOCAL HORTICULTURAL SOCIETIES with the R.H.S.

I.

Local Societies subscribing £1. 1s. per annum are entitled to—

1 Two copies of the R.H.S. *Journal*, for circulation amongst the Local Society's Members.

2. To nominate one of their Members to rank as a £1. 1s Fellow of the R.H.S., with all the privileges of a £1. 1s. Fellow, with the exception of the R.H S. *Journal*.

3 One Transferable Ticket admitting to all the R H.S. Meetings and Shows, which may be used by any Member of the Local Society.

4. To purchase, at cost price, one Silver and one Bronze Medal of the R.H S., and a printing block of Affiliation design for use on writing paper, handbills, &c.

II.

Local Societies subscribing £2. 2s. per annum are entitled to—

1. Four copies of the R.H.S. *Journal*, for circulation amongst the Local Society's Members

2. To nominate two of their Members, each to rank as a £1 1s Fellow of the R H.S., with all the privileges of £1. 1s. Fellows, excepting the *Journal*

3 Three Transferable Tickets admitting to all the R H S Meetings and Shows, which may be used by any Members of the Local Society.

4. To purchase, at cost price, two Silver and two Bronze Medals of the R.H.S., and printing block as above.

N B —Local Societies are invited to send interesting exhibits and specimens of Plants, Plant Diseases, &c., to the R.H S Fortnightly Meetings of the Floral, Fruit, Orchid, and Scientific Committees, and to correspond with the Secretary of the R H S on any interesting Horticultural subjects or events in their locality

The Secretary of the R H.S will also, at any time, be pleased to assist the Secretary of any Affiliated Society in introducing them to Horticulturists or Specialists able and willing to deliver Lectures on interesting subjects before Meetings of their Local Societies, or to act as Judges at Shows, &c , &c

Price of Medals (post free) to Affiliated Societies.

					s.	d
Silver Flora, 2½ inches in diameter, in morocco case, complete					17	9
Bronze Flora do.	do.	do.	do		6	9
Silver Banksian, 1½ inch in diameter	do	do.			8	9
Bronze Banksian do.	do.	do.	do.		4	9

Each Local Society receives a Certificate of Affiliation.

Fellows of the R H.S. belonging to Local Societies are requested to kindly call attention to the scheme of affiliation in their respective districts.

N.B.—A complete list of Local Horticultural Societies is published with the Report of the Council for 1898.

HOW TO BECOME A FELLOW
OF THE
Royal Horticultural Society.

1. Anyone interested in Horticulture is eligible for election as a Fellow, and is invited to join the Society.

2. Candidates for election are proposed by two Fellows of the Society. Forms for proposing new Fellows may be obtained at the Office, 117 Victoria Street, Westminster, or will be forwarded by post on application to the Secretary. Ladies are eligible for election as Fellows of the Society.

A Fellow subscribing 4 guineas a year (or commuting) is entitled—

1 To One Non-transferable (personal) Pass and Five Transferable Tickets admitting to all the Society's Exhibitions at the Drill Hall, Westminster, or elsewhere, and to the Chiswick Gardens on any day except Sundays

2. To attend and vote at all Meetings of the Society.

3. To the use of the Lindley Library, at the Society's Rooms, 117 Victoria Street

4 To a copy of the Society's Journal containing the Papers read at all Meetings and Conferences, Reports of Trials made at Chiswick Gardens, and descriptions and illustrations of new or rare plants, &c Back Numbers may be obtained by Fellows at half-price.

5. To purchase, at specially reduced rates, such Fruit and Vegetables as are not required for the experimental purposes of the Society.

6. To a share (in proportion to the annual subscription) of such plants, cuttings, &c, as may be available for distribution. Fellows residing beyond a radius of 35 miles distance from London (calculated by the A B C. Railway Guide) are entitled to a double share

7. Subject to certain limitations, to obtain Analysis of Manures, Soils, &c., or advice on such subjects by letter, from the Society's Consulting Chemist, Dr. J. A. Voelcker, M.A.

8. To exhibit at all Shows and Meetings, and to send seeds, plants, &c., for trial to the Society's Gardens at Chiswick.

9. To recommend any lady or gentleman for election as a Fellow of the Society.

A Fellow subscribing 2 guineas a year (or commuting) is entitled—

1 To One Non-transferable Pass and Two Transferable Tickets.

2. To the same privileges as mentioned in Nos. 2, 3, 4, 5, 6, 7, 8, 9, as above.

A Fellow subscribing 1 guinea a year (or commuting) is entitled—

1. To One Transferable Ticket (in lieu of the Non-transferable Personal Pass), and the privileges mentioned in Nos. 2, 3, 4, 5, 6, 7, 8, 9, as above.

N B.—Each Transferable Ticket or Non-Transferable Personal Pass will admit three persons to the gardens at Chiswick on any day *except* days on which an exhibition is being held, when each Ticket or Pass will admit one person only.

COMMUTATION OF SUBSCRIPTIONS.

Any Fellow wishing to commute his Annual Subscription may do so by making one payment of Forty Guineas in lieu of a £4. 4s. annual subscription; of Twenty-five Guineas in lieu of a £2. 2s. annual subscription, or of Fifteen Guineas in lieu of a £1. 1s. annual subscription; such commutation entitling the Fellow for life to all the privileges of the corresponding annual subscriptions

The Society being incorporated by Royal Charter, the Fellows incur no personal liability whatsoever, beyond the payment of their annual subscriptions.

E

THE following important and valuable Back Numbers, etc., of the "Journal" of the Royal Horticultural Society can still be obtained from the R.H.S. Offices, 117 Victoria Street, Westminster.

Vol. VII., part 2, 1886, 154 pages. Report of the PRIMULA CONFERENCE, and of the ORCHID CONFERENCE at Liverpool. To Fellows, 2s. 6d.; non-Fellows, 5s.

Vol. XI., part 3, 1889, 278 pages. Report of the NATIONAL ROSE CONFERENCE held in the SOCIETY'S GARDENS at CHISWICK. To Fellows, 2s.; non-Fellows, 5s.

Vol. XIII., part 3, 1891, 199 pages. Report of CONFERENCES on HARDY SUMMER PERENNIALS, and SMALL HARDY FRUITS. Papers on Alpine Plants, Tea Roses, Peaches and Nectarines, Stove and Greenhouse Plants, Gladioli, Insectivorous Plants, etc. To Fellows, 2s.; non-Fellows, 5s.

Vol. XIV., 1892, 588 pages. Report of the CONIFER CONFERENCE, 1891. Synopsis of the order Coniferæ, by Dr. Maxwell T. Masters; Pinetum Danicum, by Prof. Carl Hansen; Statistics of Conifers in the British Islands; Diseases of Conifers; Value of Conifers for Planting, etc., etc. Price to Fellows, 7s. 9d.; non-Fellows, 15s. 6d.

The Society's two PRIZE ESSAYS, 1895, on "HARDY FRUIT CULTURE," may be obtained from the Society's Office, 117 Victoria Street, S.W. Price 1s. 6d.

BULBOUS IRISES, by Prof. M. Foster, Secretary of the Royal Society. Profusely Illustrated. Almost every species is fully described and illustrated, and particulars as to distinguishing characteristics, growth, time of flowering, native country, etc., are given. Price 1s. 6d.

FRUITS for COTTAGERS, FARMERS, and OWNERS of SMALL GARDENS. An entirely New and greatly Revised Edition of this Pamphlet is now ready. Post free, single copy, 2d.; 25, 2s.; 50, 3s.; 100, 4s.

LaVergne, TN USA
05 December 2010
207477LV00003B/169/P